# HOW TO DRAW & PAINT IN
# WATERCOLOR & GOUACHE

## CONTENTS

# Introduction

LEARNING HOW TO draw and paint from the example and work of other artists has a long tradition, stretching back into prehistoric times. The earliest known examples are to be found in the cave paintings of southern France and Spain. The artists involved in making these images of bison and other game certainly learned their craft from example and no one would have been better qualified to give this than their more experienced elders.

The process has continued over the centuries, even though the demands of art have naturally changed. In the Middle Ages, for instance, the Church was the dominant influence on the artist, who spent much of his working life creating images to illustrate Biblical legends. Primitive man, on the other hand, probably painted as a type of magical process, hunting the beasts captured successfully on cave walls as a preparation for the actual events of the hunt. Between these two extremes came many others, from the decoration of buildings to the gratification of aristocratic whims. But, within all these approaches, there is a common core – the interpretation of the visual world.

## Learning to see
Painting and drawing are an extension of the art of seeing. It therefore follows that learning to look and see in an aware, intelligent manner is a prerequisite of good picture making. When the first attempts to draw a portrait or paint a still life prove unsatisfactory, this is just as likely to be the result of inadequate initial observation as the result of a lack of knowledge of the actual practical techniques. In any event, the cultivation of a vision of the world about you is a most rewarding and exciting experience, as well as a yardstick against which to measure the success or failure of drawings or paintings. In undertaking the process, you will be in the company of artists throughout the centuries. All of them have learned to interpret the visual world through painstaking looking, as well as through the development of basic technical skills. Study the world about you; observe the relationships of colors and the scale of things one to another – large to small, grand to insignificant. Look also at the way artists of the past saw and painted what they observed.

This process, of necessity, must be a subjective one, even though we are all part of an endless stream of development and much common ground exists from which we can learn. What will be a 'good' picture to one artist will not necessarily be so to another; a careful depiction in great detail of a favourite landscape, for instance, will be beautiful to some, but anathema to others. However, as long as the essential discipline of looking, seeing, and interpreting is observed, the basic foundations are laid for future development. The initial technological steps themselves are not always easy – and certainly can be frustrating – but it is surprising how soon the combination of a cultivated eye and a learning hand make improvements.

The eventual rewards of making telling, well-drawn and constructed drawings and paintings are great. Much pleasure and endless joy to others can ensue; the greater your experience and the wider the range of projects undertaken, the better the results. Another great benefit that springs from picture making is that you soon learn to see the world in different ways from others. The dull, olive green tone of a tree in the foreground, alongside the acid yellow greens of fresh spring foliage, will be seen to contrast well with the sun-bathed sea, shimmering turquoise blue in the middle distance. So much more can be gleaned from seeing in this way than by a casual observer.

## Learning by example
There is nothing casual, however, in preparing to make such a picture work. In the example above, the artist would distance himself from the subject and study it in terms of form, color, and inter-relationships of shapes and volumes before making even an initial mark on the board or canvas.

It would be obviously foolish to be categorical about what constitutes a sensitive line, or what makes a beautiful color harmony. These are things to be discovered out of the individual qualities of the artist. The work of the great masters of the past naturally shows such individuality and another common way of learning is to study how such artists made their pictures. Try and probe beneath the surface and discover the analytical processes and personal language at work.

Visits to galleries and, if possible, to artists' studios are always helpful. In addition, copying existing works of art can provide an invaluable insight into the mind of the original painter. This system has been used as a method of art education for a very long time. Even well-established artists both in the past and in the present make copies; indeed, the only surviving record of some very early pictures is through the copies made by later artists. Rubens (1577–1640), for instance, copied carefully a Leonardo da Vinci (1452–1519) mural. The original has long since disappeared and the work is known today only through the copy.

Often, the techniques used in the original will reveal themselves to you in making your own version of the painting or drawing. Discovering the way color is balanced, lines are put together across the canvas, perspective is drawn and character delineated will not only add to your experience but reflect back into your own work.

## Constructing a picture
When constructing a picture – constructing is the most appropriate word to describe the process – always remember that the single most important factor at the outset is the support you choose, whether it is paper, board, or canvas. The shape is significant because different shapes and proportions engender different emotions and moods. Thus a square will convey stability and solidity, while a long, narrow rectangle will suggest calm. Such horizontal rectangles are referred to as 'landscape' and vertical ones as 'portrait'. These two terms should not be confused with areas of

Left: Some of the earliest examples of drawing and painting are found in the caves of southern France. These images of bison and hunters were thought to have magical powers which promised success and prosperity.
Below: Peter Paul Rubens, 'The Judgement of Paris'. The 16th century artist Rubens was a master at rendering the figure and is well known for his fleshy, opulent nudes.

work. Constable (1776–1837), for instance, painted many landscapes on vertical canvases, while Degas (1834–1917) painted portraits on horizontal ones.

The intention of the picture – whether it is to suggest a strong sense of vigour, atmosphere, or great fidelity to the carefully observed subject – must first be decided upon, since the choice of actual working materials stems from it, together with the techniques employed.

The criterion for anything you may produce should be quality. If color is involved, then it should be harmonious, or disruptive by choice, not by accident. Balance should be aimed for in the design, but it should satisfy the viewer's need for completeness. Areas of relative inactivity can be balanced against small, tightly focused areas, where a great deal is happening. Dimensional suggestion is a further important element. The use of linear perspective and what is called atmosphere, or 'aerial perspective', to create illusions of space will also bring rewards from applied study.

## Watercolor

Watercolor is the most suitable medium for working outside the studio. Its characteristics are quite distinct from those of oils and need careful study in order to exploit them fully. The prime quality of watercolor is its transparency. It makes more use of the support – usually paper of one type and texture or another – by allowing it to shine through the thin, watered paint skins and also to describe the white, or near white, colors in the picture. This contrasts totally with the technique of working 'to the lights' used in oil painting. Because of the need to make decisions before applying the paint, it means that a great deal of discipline and organization is required, as opposed to other methods of painting.

The medium itself is an extremely old one. Frescoes, for example, are actually a form of watercolor, while watercolors on paper were being created long before the medium became popular in the 18th and 19th centuries. Part of this popularity sprang from the introduction of commercial watercolors in the 1700s. The process of manufacture itself is simple; the colors are simply powdered pigments ground in with gum arabic. Since the original method was in-

vented, various other additives have been introduced, but, though these have been found to be effective, the established formula remains the original one.

Nevertheless, the flowering of watercolor remains linked inevitably with the birth of the great watercolorist tradition in 18th century England. Artists such as John Cotman (1782–1842) and William Turner (1775–1851) brought the technique to extremely high levels. One of the more interesting elements is the scale and sense of space they achieved, given the limitation of the size of their canvases.

Most watercolor paintings are small – primarily because of the need for portability, but also due to other factors. The size of a painting is always directly related to the size of the average mark made with the medium in use. With watercolor, because of its relatively rapid drying time and the optimum amount of paint that can be carried by the brush, the commonest size is about 20in (50cm) by 30in (65cm). However, many of the finest examples are considerably smaller.

It was the artists of this period, too, who developed the classical watercolour method. This is to stretch the paper first by soaking it in clean water and then, while still wet, taping it firmly to a support, on which it is allowed to dry and tighten. This not only eliminates wrinkles and other surface blemishes; it also lifts off any grease that might be on it, via fingerprints, for instance.

### Techniques and toning

Artists of the past decided upon the mood of the scene they were painting in advance and toned their paper accordingly. This general principle is a helpful one to follow, since it serves to blend the various elements of the picture together. If the scene is to be bright, sunlit and cheerful, a very light wash of Naples yellow or yellow ochre could be used; if a heavier, overcast mood is required, a thin wash of Payne's grey or another neutral blue grey could be employed. Through this, any subsequent color will be slightly modified in tone, though not enough to prevent anything left as white appearing as white.

Most artists find the assessment and organization of tone to be the most difficult aspect of watercolor painting and, to cope with the difficulty, resort to many devices, including the squint and the white paper viewfinder.

Squinting results in a stronger definition of tonal contrasts, with mid-darks becoming darker and lights remaining strongly light. A viewfinder helps not only in ascertaining the related tones, but also the composition of the picture.

A small rectangle – the same proportion as the picture surface – is cleanly cut out of a sheet of stiff white paper. By holding it at arm's length, or closer, and closing one eye, the range of possibilities of relating objects to the picture edge can be determined. By this means, for instance, a cropped part of a tuft of grass in the foreground can be rapidly contrasted with its effect on the whole picture.

Colors are laid over the carefully organized tonal base from a limited range and in varying densities. A mellow olive green, for example, would cover most of the foliage, creating both a sense of unity and establishing the color idea. Adjustments are always made during the course of work; the answer is not simply to remove an inconvenient tree or reduce the height of a hill to make the scene tell. The whole aim is to organize the colors into an arrangement that is at once atmospheric and descriptive. Indeed, some artists believe that the melting of colors into one another is as important a part of watercolor as the quality of transparency.

## Gouache

Gouache, or body color, is included within the broad definition of watercolor. It is a water-based paint, usually made of coarsely ground pigments, but instead of having the distinctively transparent quality of pure watercolor, it is opaque.

Many techniques can be used with gouache, but a number share common ground with watercolor, oils and tempera. It should never be used as a substitute, however, since it possesses its own potential and beauty.

Using gouache on a dampened ground, for instance, creates interesting effects, as it is possible to use overlays to obliterate or qualify earlier marks. Floating semi-transparent details into a picture broadly sketched in colored inks can create a unique atmosphere, with the artist being able to use gouache alongside watercolor to contrast the latter's transparency with solid color touches. Ordinary watercolor mixed with strong opaque white can produce a similar effect.

## Composition

The illustrations created by perspective systems are a major factor in constructing a good, sound composition. Composition is the term used to express organization of varied and disparate elements within the painting to create legibility and visual interest. The balance and interrelationship of lines, masses, colors, and movement are also aspects of composition.

Over the centuries, the attempt to create standards for the making of art has taken many forms from ideal proportions for drawing the human form, to systematic color patterning.

The 'ideal', as exemplified by the Greeks as the definition of perfect proportion, was based upon a theory known as the Golden Section. This is a mathematical formula by which a line is divided in such a way that the smaller part is to the larger as the larger part is to the whole. The Golden Section was considered to hold balance naturally, entirely satisfying the human eye for symmetry and harmony. Ever since this rule was proposed, geometry has been an important and recurring concept in painting and drawing.

Atmosphere can only be sustained over the whole surface by equal consideration being given to its several parts. The basic types of composition are those based on geometry which have been used for a great many years, both in the simple and more sophisticated forms. For example, often the triangular structure found in early Madonna and Child paintings will be complemented by an inverted or interrelated triangle, sometimes to an astonishingly complex degree.

Piero della Francesca (1410/20–1492) was an Italian artist as interested in mathematics as in art but the complicated compositional structures he used did not detract from the picture's beauty and compassion. Piero is considered one of the world's greatest masters and little effort is needed to see why – not only are the linear interrelationships on the picture surface highly resolved, but color is used both logically and to enhance the aims and intentions of the picture.

These compositions are distinguished by a generally static and classical mood – an inevitable outcome of the systems used. Alternative methods have long been used and the rhythmic composition of a Rubens or

 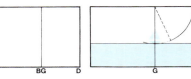

The Golden Section. This rule is ascribed to Euclid as the ideal division of a surface. Far left: To find the vertical Section, divide line AB in half to create C. Next, draw a radius from the top right corner to create D. In the next picture, draw in lines to create a rectangle. Point BG is the vertical Section. Far right: To find the horizontal Section, draw a line from the top of the vertical line G to the bottom right corner. Create a radius from the top right corner downward. Where the line and arc intersect is the horizontal Section.

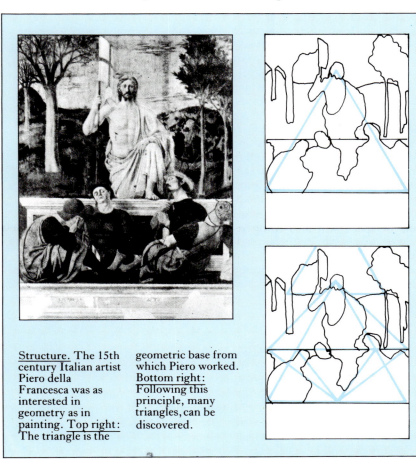

Structure. The 15th century Italian artist Piero della Francesca was as interested in geometry as in painting. Top right: The triangle is the geometric base from which Piero worked. Bottom right: Following this principle, many triangles, can be discovered.

the story use the surface and employ all available space.

### The picture space

How often has one seen pictures with the interest focused in the center, leaving corners and outer edges unoccupied, or localized nests of activity with barren and uninteresting deserts of space all around? Poussin, (1594–1665) the French painter, was greatly concerned with the grammar of composition and would invite the viewer to gain by viewing beyond the focal point all parts of the canvas.

Dramatic gesture demands balance of an asymmetrical kind. The eye needs to make space for such implied movement, in much the same way that a profile portrait will require more space between the front of the face and edge, than between the back and parallel edges.

Dramatic impact will be enhanced within the composition by a variety in scale and to this end the exploitation of close and distant viewing, not only tonally as in atmospheric perspective, but as contrasts of size on the surface. The eye of a head in close up will be seen to be approximately the same size as the full figure at a short distance behind. A sea gull in flight above Delacroix show some of them in action. In order to suggest movement, or to lead the eye across the picture surface, it is necessary to achieve balance by some other means. The interlocking of the main directional lines into a satisfactory arrangement to tell foreground cliffs will occupy the major part of the picture plane. Exploit these contrasts and use them with the other useful contributory parts.

## Color

It is necessary to study some of the basic theories of picture making and this includes perhaps the most basic, but not necessarily the simplest of all: color. No matter what other features paintings have, the common factor in all is color. Indeed, in the normally sighted human being, what is actually seen is the many and varied sensations of color. The retina of the eye receives sensations from objects which causes a reaction in the appropriate cones. As a result, trees appear green because the cones that have green as their dominant assert themselves and overcome the cones that have other colours. Similarly, the blue of the sky, is caused by the receiving of 'blue' pulses into the retina which immediately triggers a reaction to the blue-stressed cones. In color blindness these cones go wrong and often colors are reversed.

Since this complex act of seeing happens only within the brain, it is correct to deduce that nothing has color in its own right but that color is dependent upon light. In darkened conditions, colors are more difficult to see and define, and in total darkness there can be no color at all. An interesting experiment is that of creating an after-image in the retina demonstrating that it is through the brain that color is seen. Stare at a red patch, then shut your eyes and 'look' at the after-image. The same shape is seen, but in green – the complementary colour of the red patch.

Complementary colors are those at opposite sides of the color wheel. One of these colors, in this case red, reacts through the red cones and the other through the green. Taking complementary colors, we can see that a knowledge of this aspect of color theory is of value when we consider landscape painting.

In an average landscape painting, most areas are of greens of one sort or another. Brilliant, dull, acid; sage, spring, olive or sea, man has created descriptions for various conditions and types of green. If our painting comprises fields, shrubs, trees, and bushes all made up of these various greens, how better to make the harmony complete than by contrasting a

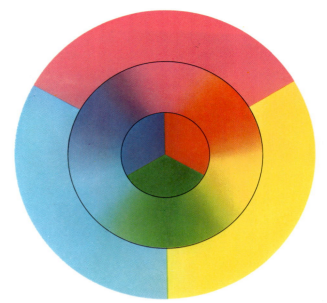

small amount of the opposite, or complementary color, being, in this instance, red. The red will serve to enhance the values of the main body of color – the range of subtly mixed greens. To expand this, since we know that green is a secondary color created from two primary colors (blue and yellow), we can begin to see how this can aid us as well. A similar effect to placing small areas of red beside the green will be created by using blue and yellow in a like manner. By using brilliant Prussian blue and raw umber or raw sienna instead of yellow, an unsuspected green tint will result. Further experimentation will reveal all manner of exciting relationships, not merely of color values – that is 'blueness' or 'redness' – but also of qualities and tones.

### Tone and hue

Color has two basic definable qualities: tone and hue. Hue is the

**The color wheel.** Color has been the subject of study for many hundreds of years ranging from the simple act of observation to highly complex psychophysical theories. In terms of painting and drawing, some of the most important terms include hue, tone, and warm and cool colors. *Hue* is the range seen in the color wheel. The *Tone* refers to the brightness of a color. *Warm and cool* colors describe the orange and blue sections of the color wheel, respectively.

**Additive mixture.** Red, green and blue are known as additive primaries. When two of these are combined a third color is created which is the complement of the third color.

**Subtractive mixture.** When two additive colors are combined they create a subtractive color. The colors produced are cyan, yellow, and magenta. When white light is passed through, black is created.

'greenness' of green paint, and tone is its darkness or lightness. Squinting is indispensable in assessing color tones when beginning to work and throughout the painting's development. Expressionistic color as used by 20th century artists such as Matisse and Derain, or the more traditional use as seen in Velazquez (17th century) are worthy of close study. In studying paintings, try always to detach the color element from the whole painting in order to examine it the better.

There is little point in simply copying 'color as seen' without attempting to first organize a scheme. Whether the artist's intention is to shock or to create a mood strictly with a number of tertiary colors, forethought is essential. One method of studying color is to use sheets of specially colored papers, cut out and placed in various shapes and combinations to see what happens when tones are too close or too distant.

## Perspective

What is a good picture? There is no simple answer; perhaps one that excites or disturbs, not one necessarily pleasing to the eye, but containing a great deal of visual interest. Not only should the artist be facile in his knowledge and use of the materials, but he or she should be conversant with these other important ingredients of visual communication and, through the fusion of these various elements, achieve his or her ambitions.

In picture making, the elements every artist needs to understand in order to best exploit them include color, composition, and perspective. The fusion of these components with a good basic drawing ability and sound technique give the artist an opportunity to express his personal vision.

These aspects of painting and drawing can be sufficiently learned to allow

One, two, and three point perspective. When two planes are visible, the parallel lines converge at a single vanishing point. When three planes are visible, two points are required. If a cube is seen above or below the horizon line, three points are used.

Seeing. The human eye functions in a highly complex system allowing us to view the world in three dimensions. Distance is formulated by the angle of convergence of the image on the retina. When many objects are viewed, sophisticated computations take place in the brain.

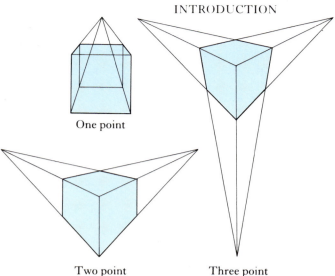

One point

Two point

Three point

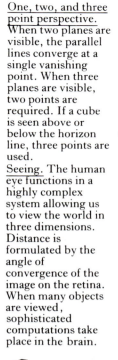

Pieter Bruegel, 'The Fall of Icarus'. The concept of aerial perspective is clearly shown in this painting. Notice how objects close up are precise and detailed and those in the middle and far distance become hazy and less well defined.

the original inspiration, no matter how ambitious, to ultimately be resolved. Systematic plotting, allied with an assertion of the artist's intention is the way to achieve good results. No one, however, should expect to always attain their highest levels of work. Being prepared to accept that the 'near

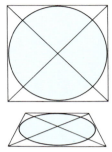

Spherical perspective. Top: If one were to visualize this shape as a teacup seen from the top, as the viewer sits down, the circle becomes an ellipse. To create an ellipse, enclose a circle in a square, bisect it, connect diagonals, and draw ellipse.

Aerial perspective. In general, objects in space diminish in tone as they recede from the viewer and those closest appear darkest. This, however, is not a hard and fast rule as many conditions will affect this principle such as the source of light, the brightness of objects and their reflected light. Tonal variations should be carefully studied rather than preconceived.

Linear and aerial perspective. The combination of linear perspective (the path) and aerial perspective (the diminishing tones of the receding trees) combine to create a sense of depth. Leonardo da Vinci created aerial perspective as a means to describe the different visible tones of objects in space. Objects viewed at a distance will appear to take on a bluish tone due to the scattering of light waves.

miss', the 'brave attempt', or even the outright failure is the sign of a good student. Experience and the ambition to push things a bit beyond one's reach is productive, sound reasoning.

Along with linear perspective, the artist uses aerial or atmospheric perspective. Aerial perspective is that which deals with the reduction and changes of tones and colors due to the distance between them and the viewer. A formula used in the past, e.g., by Pieter Bruegel (c.1525–1569) in 'The Fall of Icarus', demonstrates the basic idea of aerial perspective. Objects close-up are seen to be in full tonal and color values; bright, light surfaces facing the light source, and dark in those turned away. Objects

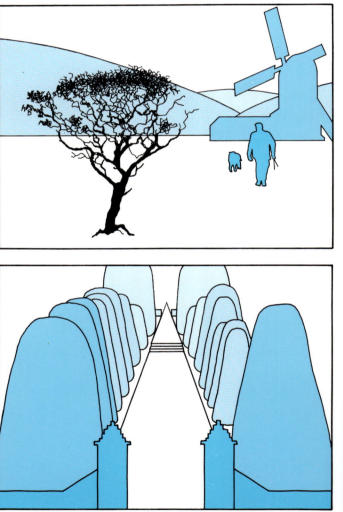

seen at a short distance, behind these objects, can be seen to have a less well defined distinction between their light and dark sides.

In atmospheric perspective, colors will be seen to have been modified by the atmosphere and to take on a bluish tone. In the middle distance, this is more marked with less subject definition and closer color values, and so on until, in the far distance, only the shape of objects can be discerned and the blue so assertive that things appear to be pure blue. This use of the dark brown foreground, green middle distance, and blue far-distance was in common use in the 17th and 18th centuries. No such rigid formula is to be encouraged, but the use of aerial perspective is essential in the type of work under discussion.

The simplest demonstration of the problems encountered by anyone attempting to transfer a sphere on to a two-dimensional surface is seen in that of two-dimensional projections of the earth. One can begin to see that the point of using such a system of perspective is simply to allow the picture to tell its intended truth. The artist, however, must understand the limitation of such theories well enough to be prepared to depart from the rules as much as needed.

This is of course a direct corollary to the embracing of any scientific method be it of color, perspective, or proportions. They are very useful as servants, potentially disastrous as masters. The one constant criterion in all picture making is the intention and content of the work undertaken; all other considerations are dependent upon this. A good artist is prepared to use all, or none, of these systems towards this end.

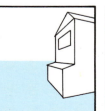

The horizon line. The horizon line is always at eye level. No matter what the size or dimensions of objects, their diagonal lines will all converge on the horizon line.

To visualize the scale of a painting, when studying the techniques used, each of the pictures shown from pages 12 to 61 are illustrated on a small grid to show their relative size. The maximum size being 39in × 30in (97cm × 75cm), each square in the grid represents 3in (7.5cm). The relative size of the painting is indicated by the tinted area.

Albrecht Durer: The Monumental Turf. Durer was the first major artist to use water colour.

# Watercolor

WATERCOLOR IS ONE of the most versatile of drawing media. It can be handled with precision for fine detail work but is also naturally suited to a fluid and spontaneous style. You can exploit random effects in the flow and fall of the paint by spattering color from the end of the brush or blowing the thin, wet washes into irregular rivulets across the paper. Integrate these marks with carefully controlled brushwork to vary the textures in the painting.

The full effect of watercolor depends upon luminous, transparent washes of color built up layer upon layer. As white paint deadens the freshness of color, small areas of highlight are achieved by leaving the white paper bare while light tones are produced by using thin washes of color. Dark tones are slowly brought to a suitable intensity by the use of several successive applications of thin layers of the same color.

The urn shape was initially protected with a layer of masking fluid, painted carefully into the outline. This seals off the paper while the rest of the surface is freely painted over with large brushes and watery paint. When the work is complete and dry you can then rub off the mask and work on shadows and highlights of the shape with a small brush.

## Materials

**Surface**
Heavy stretched paper

**Size**
23in × 20in (40cm × 50cm)

**Tools**
2B pencil
No 6 sable round brush
No 10 ox-eye round brush
1in (2.5cm) decorators' brush
Masking fluid

**Colors**

| | |
|---|---|
| Burnt umber | Hooker's green |
| Cadmium red medium | Ivory black |
| Chrome green | Payne's grey |
| Cobalt blue | Yellow ochre |

**1.** Sketch in the basic lines of the drawing with a pencil, carefully outlining the shape of the urn. Paint in this shape with masking fluid and let it dry completely.

**2.** Use a No 10 ox-eye brush to lay a broad light wash of cobalt blue across the top half of the painting and chrome green and Payne's grey across the foreground.

**3.** Mix a dark, neutral grey and paint wet streaks of color to form the trunks of the trees. Blow the wet paint in strands across the paper making a network of branches.

**4.** As the paint dries, work over the structure with green, grey and umber rolling the brush into the pools of paint and letting the color spread.

**5.** Load a decorators' brush with paint and flick tiny spots of colour into the washes. Block in the shape of the wall with a thin layer of red and brown using a No 6 brush.

**6.** Work over the foreground with the decorators' brush loaded with Hooker's green, using a rough, scrubbing motion. Draw in details on the wall.

**7.** Let the painting dry completely. Gently rub away the masking fluid with your finger – make sure all the fluid is off and try not to damage the paper.

**8.** Paint in the shadows on the urn in brown and grey, adding a little yellow ochre and light red to warm the tones. Paint the form and stonework.

# Masking fluid · spattering · blotting · stippling

To create a spattered effect, load a large bristle brush with paint and quickly run your finger or a small knife through the hairs.

An alternative to spattering paint is to stipple with the end of a broad bristle brush. Here the artist is using a decorators' brush to lay in small dots of color.

A dense, leafy texture can be achieved by blotting a wet area with a piece of tissue. Do not rub but simply put the tissue down, press, and pick it up to leave small gaps and crevices in the paint surface.

Masking fluid may be used to protect the white paper from the paint. When the painting is completed, rub off the fluid with your finger. If the fluid is put on with a brush, make sure to rinse the brush immediately after use.

THE TECHNIQUES REQUIRED for this type of painting are quite lengthy and it is advisable to practise on scraps of a similar paper before beginning the actual painting.

A large, wet pool of color will dry with a gradated tone and strong, irregular outline. Overlaying a succession of washes produces vivid colors, a patterned network of light and dark tones, and linear detail suggesting the texture of foliage and flowers. You can speed up the drying process with a hairdryer or fan but, since this tends to deaden the color, it is best to let the painting dry naturally.

The image is built up in the traditional watercolor technique of working from light to dark. Start by laying in pale tones in thin, broad washes leaving patches of white paper to form highlight areas. Because the paint is so fluid, only one good-quality, medium-sized sable brush is needed. Make broad sweeps of watery color with the bristles loose or spread, and bring the tip to a point for finer details. Study each shape carefully and draw directly with the brush. Color can be lifted from the surface with a clean, damp Q-tip to lighten the tones. Detailed corrections are difficult with this type of painting, but it is possible to make small corrections by rubbing the surface when completely dried with a fine-grained sandpaper.

## Materials

Surface
Stretched white cartridge paper

Size
13in × 8in (32cm × 20cm)

Tools
HB pencil
No 6 round sable brush
Plate or palette
Q-tips

Colors
| | |
|---|---|
| Alizarin crimson | Emerald green |
| Black | Prussian blue |
| Burnt sienna | Scarlet lake |
| Cadmium yellow | Viridian |
| Cobalt blue | Yellow ochre |

Medium
Water

**1.** Sketch out the composition very lightly with an HB pencil. Lay washes of thin wet paint to establish basic forms and local colors.

**2.** Work over the painting again with light washes blocking in more shapes. Let the colors run together in patches to create a soft, fuzzy texture.

## Cleaning with knife · sanding · blotting

Where paint has inadvertently splashed on the white surface, the artist can very carefully scratch it off with a knife.

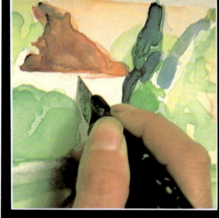

After scraping off spots or splashes, the artist is here very lightly sanding the surface with a fine grade sandpaper. Use a very light touch.

**3.** Let the painting dry and then apply layers of denser color, gradually building up the forms with thin overlays.

**4.** Paint in the shadow shapes over the grass with broad streaks of blue and green. Work into the trees with overlapping areas of colour to show the form.

**5.** Strengthen dark tones in the background with Prussian blue and black. Lay a broad wash of yellow over the grass to lift the tone.

To lighten a tone or stop the paint from bleeding, a Q-tip can be used to blot up excess moisture or color. This can also be used to blend colors.

# Gouache

THIS PAINTING demonstrates an innovative and imaginative method of combining gouache with another water-based medium – ink – to create an individual and expressive seascape. There is nothing innovative in the use of an underpainting in itself, but it is not generally used with water-based media such as watercolor or gouache due to the inherent transparency of these media. In this instance, the artist has first executed an underpainting in bold, primary colors, which serves to unify the painting and help eliminate the inevitable chalkiness of gouache.

Since the more traditional method of underpainting requires time-consuming layering of color upon color, the use of these bold colors for the underpainting expedites the painting process. In this method, the artist can jump directly from the underpainting to developing the basic structure of the painting without having to wait for previous coats to dry.

While opaque and flat, gouache retains many of the qualities of all water-based paints and can be worked wet-into-wet, spattered, or dry-brushed. The artist has here used a combination of all of these techniques which, when combined with a subtle mixture of color and tone – all of which are enhanced by the initial underpainting – results in an evocative and atmospheric painting.

## Materials

Surface
Stretched watercolor paper

Size
19in × 17in (47cm × 42.5cm)

Tools
Nos 4, 6, 10 sable brushes
Palette or mixing plate
Tissues or rags

Colors

| Gouache: | Colored inks: |
|----------|---------------|
| Black | Black |
| Burnt umber | Blue |
| Olive green | Green |
| Payne's grey | Orange |
| Prussian blue | Red |
| White | |

Medium
Water

## Underpainting with ink · details

The very bold colors of an underpainting done in colored inks will later be modified by opaque gouache. Here, in the first step, (below) the inks are bleeding into one another.

**1.** With a No 10 brush, lay down broad areas of red, orange, blue and green ink corresponding to the shapes and color tones of the subject.

**2.** While still wet, mix a variety of grey tones from white, olive green, and Payne's grey gouache. Very loosely rough in the pier allowing the ink and gouache to bleed.

**3.** With a No 4 brush, begin to dot in lighter tones of grey and white, once again allowing the colors to bleed together.

**4.** Cover the orangish underpainting in the foreground with a thin wash of burnt umber.

**5.** Add a touch of olive green to the white, Payne's grey, and green mixture and with the No 10 brush cover the sky and sea area with broad, loose strokes.

**6.** Cover the remaining sky area in this same color and let dry. Using pure white gouache, block in white shape to left and small touches of white in the foreground.

In the final steps, the artist puts in small details of pure black gouache with a small sable brush.

**7.** Add more olive green to the mixture and loosely put in strokes in sea and foreground rocks. Put pure white on a No 4 brush and spatter.

**8.** With a No 4 brush and black gouache, put in the fine details of the picture.

NO ONE MEDIA can completely capture the diverse and subtle range of colors to be found in nature; the total effect is created by the relationships of all the colors together and the influence of light. Even if a landscape is predominantly green, there are a multitude of tones and hues within the one color to be identified and translated onto the painting surface. A low-key green, for example, may be caused by a subtle cast of blue or red and the painting will be livelier if these contrasts are exploited or exaggerated.

As a general rule, remember that colors in the foreground are the most intense and fade towards the horizon. Within this range there are shifts between warm and cool tones; these help to establish form and position in the overall scheme of the painting.

Only one brush and a limited color range have been used for this painting; the variety of hues and tones is due to careful, observant color mixing. As gouache is thick and opaque, be careful not to overmix the colors. The paint can be laid in thin washes of color or thickly daubed depending on how much water is added.

## Materials

Surface
Stretched heavy cartridge paper

Size
14.5in × 18in (36cm × 45cm)

Tools
No 6 round sable brush

Colors
Brilliant green     Cobalt blue
Black     Scarlet
Cadmium yellow     White

Medium
Water

1. Paint in soft shapes to show trees, sky and water using thin washes of blue and green adding white to vary the tone.

2. Work into these colors with darker tones to establish the basic forms and give the impression of distance.

3. With undiluted paint, overpaint the forms in detail, varying the green hues by adding touches of yellow or red. Intensify the colors in the reflections on the water.

4. Mix brown from scarlet and black and draw up the trunk and branches of the tree. Extend the shape of the tree working with small dabs of red, green and orange.

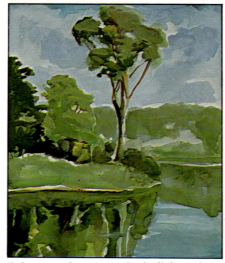

5. Increase the contrast in the light and dark colors over the whole image. Work into the foreground with horizontal and vertical stripes of blended color.

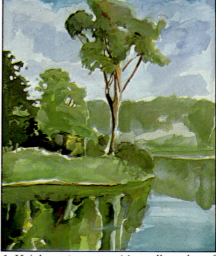

6. Heighten the tones with small patches of thin paint over the sky and trees, mixing white into the colors.

# Highlighting

Working over a partially dry underpainting, the artist puts in a highlight tone.

# Watercolor

THE WATERCOLOR techniques used for this painting are particularly well suited to the subject. A combination of loose transparent strokes with opaque white gouache produce an interesting contrast in both texture and tone.

The techniques used – working wet-in-wet and dry-brush – require that the painting be executed quickly and confidently. The process involves working from dark to light and from the general to the particular.

Tinted paper was chosen since it has a unifying and reinforcing effect on the painting. When the color of the paper is used as a 'color' within the subject, as demonstrated in the head of the bird, the contrast in color and texture both heighten the interest in the subject and link it to its environment.

The method of painting is largely intuitive: you should try and let the painting develop independently and take advantage of the various movements of the paint on the surface. A careful combination of control and a willingness to take chances is required and you should learn to take advantage of 'accidents' and use them to express the unique qualities of the picture.

## Materials

**Surface**
Heavy watercolor paper stretched on board

**Size**
15in × 22in (37.5cm × 55cm)

**Tools**
Board
Gummed tape
Nos 1 and 2 sable watercolor brushes
Tissues or rags

**Colors**
Alizarin crimson          Payne's grey
Cadmium red medium   Prussian blue

**Medium**
Water

**1.** With a 2B pencil, lightly sketch in the subject. With a No 2 sable brush, lay in a thin wash of burnt umber, blue, and alizarin crimson to define the shape of the bird.

**2.** Mix a small amount of white gouache with blue and lay this over the undercolors, thinning with water. Put in dark areas with Payne's grey.

**3.** With a No 1 brush, mix white gouache with blue and touch in feathers with a light, directional stroke. Add more blue and describe feather texture in the wing.

## Underpainting: feathering with brush tip

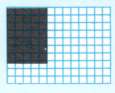

(**A**, <u>above</u>) The artist puts in a cool underpainting with a wet wash and large sable brush.

(**B**, <u>above</u>) Using the dry-brush technique, the artist describes a feather texture in the neck.

(**C**, <u>below</u>) With a small sable brush and pure white, detail highlights are put in, the final stage.

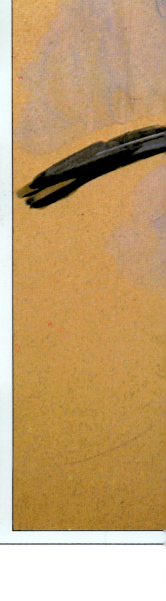

**4.** With the same brush mix an opaque mixture of Payne's grey and blue and carefully put in dark details of the wings, tail, and head.

**5.** With a clean, dry No 1 brush pick up a small amount of white gouache. Feather this onto the bird's breast and throat in a quick, flicking motion.

**6.** With a very thin wash of white gouache mixed with blue, quickly rough in the shadow area around the bird.

WATERCOLOR USES transparency to create both color and tone. For this reason white is not normally a part of the watercolorist's palette and thus the artist must rely on the various techniques and color mixes to achieve a successful picture. In this painting the variety of techniques illustrate the flexibility of the medium, as well as the skill required to use it to its best potential.

The demands of using watercolor require that the artist be able to anticipate what will happen in advance of putting the paint on the surface. This can be a hit or miss effort, especially when applying loose washes of color or letting colors bleed into one another. The artist has a certain amount of control over where and how the paint is applied, but once the brush touches the paper there is much that can happen which the artist will not be able to predict.

In this case, while care was taken to capture a true representation of the subject, the background was described in a more or less *ad hoc* manner, allowing paint and water to mix with no attempt to control its movement on the surface.

**1.** Mix a very wet wash of cadmium green and water and loosely define the leaf shapes with a No 6 brush.

**2.** With a small amount of cerulean blue and a No 2 brush, put in the dark areas of the flowers. Mix green and yellow ochre and lay in the dark areas of the leaves.

## Materials

Surface
Stretched watercolor paper

Size
23in × 18in (57cm × 45cm)

Tools
Nos 2, 6, 10 sable brushes
1½ (3.75cm) housepainting brush
Palette

Colors
| | |
|---|---|
| Black | Payne's grey |
| Cadmium green | Vermilion |
| Cerulean blue | Yellow ochre |

Medium
Water

**3.** Mix a large, wet amount of Payne's grey, cerulean blue, and water. With a No 10 brush, put in the background. Keep the paint very wet as you work.

**4.** With a No 2 brush, develop dark tones of the leaves by mixing Payne's grey with green. Again, keep the mixture wet and let colours bleed into one another.

**5.** With a No 2 brush, apply details of stems and veins in pure Payne's grey.

## Finished picture · creating leaf shapes · overpainting flowers

To bring the picture together and make it more interesting, in the final stages the artist concentrated on darkening and strengthening the overall image. The background was brought down to describe the foreground plane, and leaves and flowers were touched up with stronger tones.

With a very wet wash of water and green, the artist describes the general leaf shapes. The wet paint is pulled out of these areas in thin strands to create the stems of the leaves.

With a small sable brush the artist is here touching in areas of deep red over the lighter underpainting. From a distance, this will give the flowers depth and texture.

ANY WATERCOLOR study of this kind is an exercise in drawing with color. In both objects, by carefully copying each detail of color and texture, the whole impression of the form slowly emerges. The shell is delicately tinged with red, yellow, and grey and the subtle tonal changes which occur as the light falls over the undulating surface are subtly indicated.

Lay in broad washes of basic color to show the simple form and contour of the objects. Pick out linear details such as the network of triangular shapes on the pine cone, drawing with the point of a small sable brush. Use thin washes of color to describe the pools of shadow and natural tints of the shell. Keep the paint smooth and liquid but do not overload the brush – the color should flow freely but not flood the drawing. The work should be dried before fine lines are added otherwise they will fan out and lose precision. Brush wet washes of color together to blend the hues and make the paint spread into soft, blurred shapes of variegated tone. Mix up a subtle range of browns and greys to vary the dark tones and drop in touches of pure color to highlight the surface patterns.

## Materials

Surface
Thick cartridge paper

Size
13in × 15in (32cm × 37.5cm)

Tools
Nos 4, 8 sable round brushes
Palette

Colors
Black                  Gamboge yellow
Burnt sienna           Payne's grey
Burnt umber            Scarlet lake
Cobalt blue

Medium
Water

**1.** Draw the shape of the pine cone with the tip of a No 4 brush and lay in a light wash of burnt umber. Vary the tone with touches of Payne's grey.

**2.** Work lightly over the shape of the shell following the local color. Pick out small surface details on both objects.

**3.** Develop the texture and pattern in each shape, drawing fine lines and small patches of color with the point of the brush in dark tones of grey and brown.

**4.** Strengthen the dark tone inside the mouth of the shell and continue to work over the pine cone, using the direction of the brushmarks to describe the forms.

**5.** Lay thin washes of grey, brown and red into the shape of the shell with a No 8 brush.

**6.** Work over both objects with line and wash until the patterns are complete.

# Pine cone details · shell tones

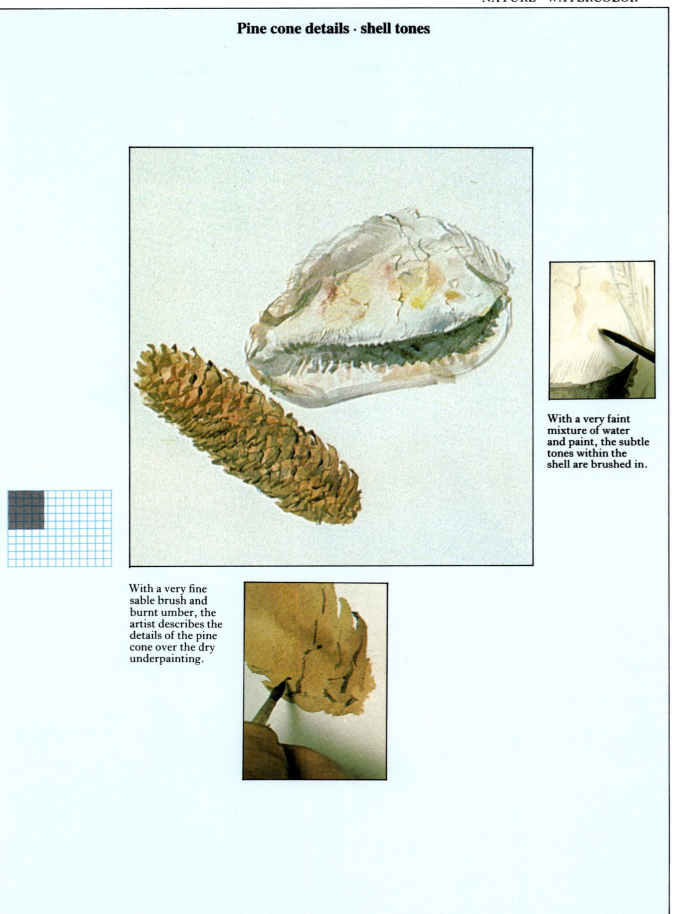

With a very faint mixture of water and paint, the subtle tones within the shell are brushed in.

With a very fine sable brush and burnt umber, the artist describes the details of the pine cone over the dry underpainting.

WATERCOLOR IS AT its best when used for subjects requiring sensitivity and delicacy. In this case, the use of watercolor goes far in developing an appropriate aqueous and 'watery' image.

The techniques used by the water-colorist are many and not a few are invented on the spot as the artist is working. There is no formula for creating a successful watercolor painting; however, the better acquainted the artist is with the nature of the medium, the more he will be able to pick and choose – and invent – the techniques most suitable to create an interesting and expressive picture.

In developing this picture, the artist has depended largely on two methods of painting. In some areas he has used the classical wet-into-wet technique – that is, flooding one area of color into another while still wet; in other areas he has laid down a small area of color and then flooded this with water. The combination of the two from the earlier techniques makes the finished painting more interesting than if it were limited to one type only. It is the combination of broad, loose areas of pale color contrasted with smaller, tighter areas of dark detail which give the subject its mystery and interest. Without this contrast and harmonious balance between loose and tight, dark and light, the picture would not be so successful in holding the observer's attention or capturing the essence of the subject.

## Materials

Surface
Heavy watercolor paper stretched on board

Size
22in × 15in (55cm × 37.5cm)

Tools
Nos 2 and 6 sable watercolor brushes
Tissues or rags

Colors
Alizarin crimson    Payne's grey
Cadmium red medium   Prussian blue

Medium
Water

**1.** On a piece of stretched paper, dampen the shape of the fish with water. With a small sable brush put in a thin wash of blue and purple. Flood with brush and water.

**2.** Redampen the area to be worked on. With a fine brush and dryish paint, put in the head and spine details in Payne's grey letting this bleed into the other colors.

## Wet-in-wet · dark details the wash

With a fine sable brush, the artist puts in fine lines of color over slightly damp paper.

Putting in dark details in the head with a dryish paint mixture. The color is then flooded with water and a clean brush to make it bleed.

**3.** After allowing the previous layer to dry slightly, use a stronger and darker mixture of Payne's grey to further define the head.

**4.** Mix a thin wash of purple and yellow and apply lightly over the body of the fish. Blot with tissue if too wet.

**5.** Using the deep Payne's grey mixture and a small brush, put in the pattern on the back and heighten tail details.

Working over dark areas with a thin wash of color. When a wet layer is applied over a dried area, a transparent effect is achieved allowing the first color to blend and show through the second.

# Gouache

BECAUSE OF their varied textures, colors, and shapes, plants can be an interesting subject for a painting.

To make an effective color study of one plant, arrange it in a well-lit position, preferably against a plain background. Sit far enough away to be able to see the whole form, as otherwise the shapes may become distorted in the drawing. You can move to take a closer look at the details whenever necessary. First draw the whole plant in outline and then start to apply colors. A successful rendering depends upon careful observation of the color relationships as a whole – each hue and tone is modified by its surroundings. Be prepared to make continual alterations to the colors and shapes.

In this example the initial drawing was made in charcoal. The soft, dusty black creates a strong structure for the work and is easy to correct or overpaint. Keep the charcoal drawing clean, or the fine black powder will mix into the paint and deaden the colors. Lay in thin colors at the start to establish general tones and then work over each shape to revise the colors and build up the pattern.

## Materials

Surface
Stretched white cartridge paper

Size
15in × 19in (37.5cm × 47cm)

Tools
No 6 round sable brush
Willow charcoal
Plate or palette

Colors
Black
Cadmium yellow medium
Cyprus green
May green

Olive green
Raw umber
Scarlet lake
White

Medium
Water

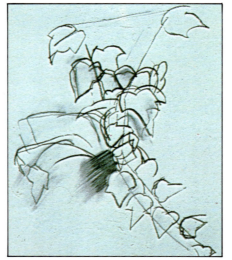

**1.** Draw up the outline with charcoal showing the shapes of the leaves and the stalks. Work freely, correcting where necessary by rubbing lightly over the lines.

**2.** Brush away excess charcoal dust from the surface of the drawing and with a No 6 brush work into the leaves to show the green patterning.

**3.** Fill in the whole shape of each leaf. Draw the stalks of the plant in red using the tip of the brush.

**4.** Revise the drawing with charcoal and paint over alterations with white. Continue to develop the colors, putting in a darker tone behind the leaves.

**5.** Build up the image piece by piece with applied color, gradually adding to the detail and refining the shapes.

**6.** Adjust the tones of the colors to draw out the natural contrasts. Complete each shape before moving onto the next.

## Negative shapes · spattering

A good example of the use of negative shapes. Here the artist creates the white lines in the jacket by describing the red areas around them rather than by painting the lines.

Spattering to create texture. Using a decorator's brush, the artist holds the brush above the paper and taps it lightly to create a tonal effect.

THE ARTIST can learn as much, if not more, from working with a limited palette and simple subject as he can from using many colors and a complicated subject.

This type of painting can be more difficult than painting on a large or complex scale as the artist is required to study carefully the subject in order to see minute variations in shape, tone, and color. You will discover that shadows are not merely areas of grey, but include very slight color differentiations and barely perceptible variations in tone. You will see how a simple piece of lettuce – which most people would describe as 'leafy green' – is in reality made up of many colors, tiny veins of light, and reflections.

An interesting experiment is to make the subject larger than real life. This type of work takes great concentration but the rewards are many. You will find that when you move on to more complex subjects, you will use what you have learned while working in detail on simple subjects.

## Materials

Surface
Watercolor pad

Size
10in × 12in (25cm × 30cm)

Tools
No 2 sable watercolor brush
Plate or palette

Colors
Light red
Ultramarine blue
Viridian green
Yellow ochre

Medium
Water

**1.** Draw in the design with a No 2 sable brush and ultramarine blue.

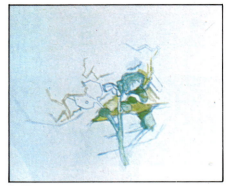

**2.** Using just enough water to keep the paint flowing, develop a small area of the picture and then carry this color over to a new area.

## Finished picture · outlining · working in new area

To finish off the picture (<u>right</u>), the artist laid a blue wash around the left side, running over and into the lettuce shape. This served to heighten blue tones within the lettuce and contrast with the red outside.

With a fine point sable brush, the artist begins by working over the preliminary pencil sketch with a thin wash of blue.

**3.** Using varying tones of yellow ochre, light red, viridian, and blue, work over the entire picture. Work back and forth between new and old areas.

**4.** Working into the outlined area with a wash of greens, develop a contrast between the lettuce and other leaves with different shades of green.

**5.** Strengthen outlines in blue and red. The red outline contrasts with the predominant blues and greens of the subject. Leave the white of the paper.

The artist worked in small areas, one at a time. Here the completed area can be seen and the artist is now describing the blue outline for the next area to be painted.

IT IS NOT always necessary to go to great lengths to assemble a still life as a small, ordinary object such as a teabag offers a complex structure and intricate range of tones and colors. As well, practice in quick watercolor studies develops keen perception and skills in drawing and painting which are a sound basis for work in any medium.

Here watercolor is used for a study which is essentially direct and immediate. The painting is rapidly completed, building up the form with a combination of line and thin washes of paint; the subject emerges through a careful interpretation of tiny shapes of color and tone.

In small paintings of this kind, the paint should be wet but not overly so, ensuring that the marks are easy and fluid but controlled. The final effect is achieved by constantly checking lines and shapes; working wash over line; and drawing back into the washes. A limited range of color is used to create a variety of tones, demonstrating the rich versatility and potential of watercolors.

## Materials

Surface
Cartridge paper

Size
7in × 10in (17cm × 25cm)

Tools
No 2 round watercolor brush

Colors

| | |
|---|---|
| Black | Prussian blue |
| Cobalt blue | Viridian |
| Light red | Yellow ochre |

Medium
Water

**1.** Load the brush with Prussian blue paint, well thinned with water. Draw the outline of the shape and details of the form with the point of the brush.

**3.** Let the painting dry and then start to define the shapes with washes of light red. Overlay red on blue to bring out the form.

**5.** Draw into the washes of paint with a stronger tone of light red to describe creases in the surface. Indicate the shape of the plate with a light wash of viridian.

**2.** Block in shadow areas with thin washes of cobalt blue. The color should not be too too strong as this is the basis of a series of overlaid layers of paint.

**4.** Continue to work with light red, cooling the tone where necessary with yellow ochre. Add definition to the shadows with blue washes in and around the outlines.

**6.** Where the color is too strong, lighten with a brush dipped in clean water. When the surface is dry, draw up the outlines again in blue with the point of the brush.

# Initial washes · redefining outlines

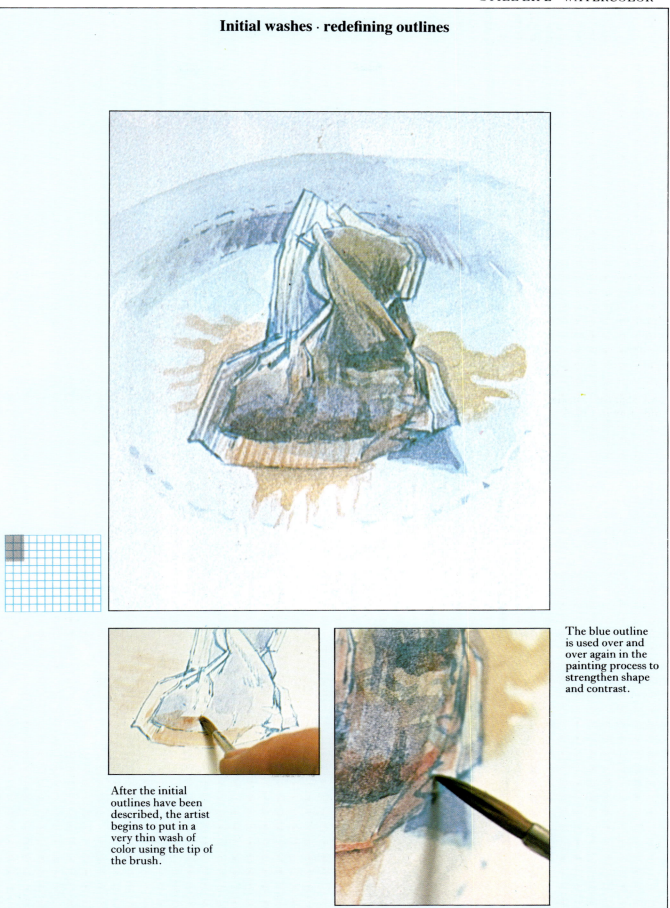

The blue outline is used over and over again in the painting process to strengthen shape and contrast.

After the initial outlines have been described, the artist begins to put in a very thin wash of color using the tip of the brush.

# Gouache

GOUACHE IS a water-based paint but thicker and more opaque than watercolor. The colors are clear and bright; mixed with white they create sparkling pastel tints. Use thick paint straight from the tube to overlay strong colors, or thin it with water to flood in light washes.

At first glance this painting may appear to be carefully detailed and realistic but, as the steps show, the technique is fluid and informal. The first step, for example, is not a meticulous drawing but a mass of vivid, liquid pools of color suggesting basic forms. As the paint is laid on in layers of loose streaks and patches, the impression of solidity and texture gradually emerges. Each object is described by carefully studying the subject colors and translating these into the painting.

In general, the technique used for this painting was to thicken the paint slightly with each application; but thin washes are laid in the final stage to indicate textures and shadows. The combination of thin washes with flat, opaque patches of color is most effective in capturing the reflective surface of the bottle and glass.

## Materials

**Surface**
Stretched cartridge paper

**Size**
12.5in × 17in (31cm × 45cm)

**Tools**
No 12 flat ox-ear brush
Nos 5, 8 round sable brushes
Plate or palette

**Colors**

| | |
|---|---|
| Burnt umber | Sap green |
| Cadmium yellow | Yellow ochre |
| Magenta | White |

**Medium**
Water

**1.** With a No 8 sable brush lay in the basic shapes of the objects with thin, wet paint. Use burnt umber, sap green, magenta and yellow and let the color flow together.

**2.** With a No 5 brush, put in yellow ochre around the shapes and into the foreground. Work over the bottle and loaf of bread, painting in shadow details.

**3.** Indicate shadows in the background with a thin layer of green. Apply small patches of solid color to show form and surface texture in each object.

**4.** With a No 12 brush, block in small dabs and streaks of color, developing the tones and textures.

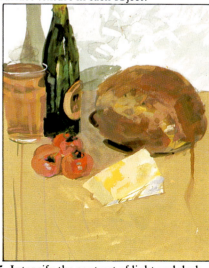

**5.** Intensify the contrast of light and dark with white highlights and brown shadows with the No 5 brush. Work into the background with white.

**6.** Work over the foreground and background with light tones of pink and yellow, keeping the paint thin. Spatter brown and black over the loaf.

# Painting wet-in wet · overpainting dry surface · using paint from tube

**A.** After dampening the paper in the shape of the object with water, the artist lays in a wash of color, allowing it to bleed over the damp area.

**B.** Over the dry underpainting, the artist here blocks in the label on the bottle with dryish paint.

**C.** Using paint directly from the tube and a large brush well loaded with water, the background is blocked in.

# Watercolor

IN THIS PAINTING, strong patterns of light and shade introduce an abstract element to an otherwise straightforward pose. The tone and color contrasts form an intricate network of shapes which are emphasized to build up the image piece by piece. The figure is basically composed of warm tones of orange, yellow, and brown and are given extra brilliance by the cool, dark blues of surrounding colors. These colors are linked across the image with the warm mauve and intense blue-purple in the shadows of the figure and the background. The strong green of the floor is an unexpected departure from the overall color scheme and provides a lively base for the composition.

The painting technique is fluid and vigorous. Large pools of color are laid down to establish the general shapes, which are then broken down by successive applications of smaller patches of wet color. Use round sable brushes with a relaxed, flowing stroke; a great part of the appeal of the image is that no shape is absolutely precise. To make the most of the colors, dry the painting frequently so that the effect of the overlapping washes is not diffused.

## Materials

Surface
Stretched cartridge paper

Size
9.5in × 15in (24cm × 37cm)

Tools
No 5 sable round brush
Colored pencils    2B pencil

Colors

| | |
|---|---|
| Burnt umber | Scarlet lake |
| Cadmium yellow | Ultramarine blue |
| Cobalt blue | *Pencils* |
| Emerald green | Blue |
| Orange | Orange |
| Purple | Purple |
| Magenta | |

Medium
Water

**1.** Sketch in a rough guideline for the painting with a 2B pencil. Lay in shadows with thin washes of paint using warm colors.

**2.** Work into the figure with yellow and violet developing the pattern of light and shade. Put in the floor with a wash of emerald green, blues and purples.

**3.** Build up the contrast of warm and cool tones in the figure, blocking in small patches of color to describe shadows.

**4.** Mix the paint with less water to intensify the dark tones. Break down the large shapes to show details such as facial features and the fingers on the hand.

**5.** Work over the skin tones with small shapes of burnt sienna and burnt umber. Overlap the colors and drop in touches of blue to vary the dark tones.

**6.** When the paint is dry, work over the forms with colored pencils, modifying the shapes and tones.

# Lifting color with tissue · overlaying with colored pencils

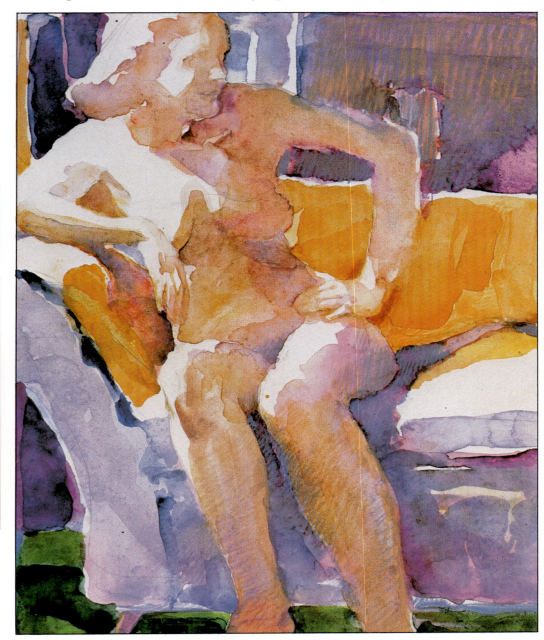

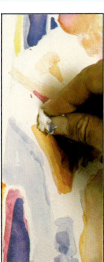

To lighten a color tone, a small piece of tissue can be used to lift the paint. Do not rub into the surface but simply blot with the tissue.

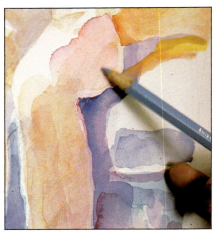

After the painting has dried, colored pencils may be used to create subtle overlays of color. Here the artist strengthen shadow areas in the legs using a blue pencil over a warm color area.

WATERCOLOR IS AN excellent medium for painting a nude, as its delicacy and transparency are particularly suited to the task of building up subtle variations of flesh tones. Color is gradually intensified and broken down into smaller areas with light tones created by the bare white surface of the paper.

To create a balanced composition, the figure has been placed to one side of the paper with the head turned to look across the picture space. The dark, heavy background area adds emphasis to light colors and details within the figure. The model's hat gives a splash of bright color against the subtle flesh tones and cool blue and grey of the surrounding area.

The success of this type of painting depends upon accurate, direct drawing with a good sable brush. Work on each form separately to build up details and make adjustments in the final stages to unify the overall effect. Each shape should be carefully observed and then precisely applied. Keep the paint thin and light as it is difficult to lift off color which has been applied too thickly. It is advisable to dry the painting frequently by either letting the moisture evaporate naturally, fanning the picture, or using a hair dryer so the colors do not mix and become muddy. Brushes should be kept clean and water pots refilled at regular intervals during the work.

## Materials

**Surface**
Stretched watercolor paper

**Size**
20in × 16in (50cm × 40cm)

**Tools**
Nos 3 and 6 sable round brushes
No 10 flat ox-ear brush
1in (2.5cm) decorators' brush

**Colors**

| | |
|---|---|
| Black | Cobalt blue |
| Burnt sienna | Light red |
| Cadmium red | Payne's grey |
| Cadmium yellow | Scarlet lake |

**Medium**
Water

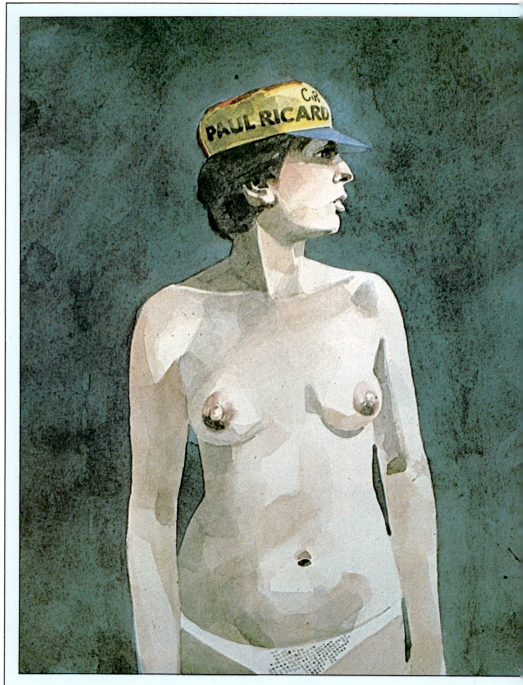

## Detailing with pencil

A fine-pointed, dark pencil is here being used to create texture and pattern in the model's pants.

**1.** Lightly pencil in the outline of the figure and with a No 3 brush paint in the darkest details with black. Lay in a very thin wash of light red with a No 10 brush.

**2.** Paint in small areas of bright pattern on the cap, keeping the colors clean and distinct. With a No 3 brush and black, brush into the cap to indicate shadows.

**3.** Gradually build up skin tones with thin washes of paint, varying the color mixtures and overlaying washes.

**4.** Use a large No 6 brush to apply a wash of color across the background, with a mixture of cobalt blue and Payne's grey. Follow the outline of the figure carefully.

**5.** Strengthen the shadows in the figure, preserving highlights and light tones. Lay light washes of scarlet lake.

**6.** Intensify the background color, adding a little black to the blue and grey mixture.

**7.** Adjust the tones of the figure against the dark background, bringing up details of the features and adding small shapes of dark color to show strong shadows.

**8.** Work over the whole image to define the full volume of the head and body, using thin washes of black and red to sharpen detail and enliven color.

THE ATMOSPHERIC MOOD of this picture was achieved through the subtle overlaying of washes of color and a dramatic use of light and shadow.

Within the figure, this method of painting mimics the actual physical makeup of the human body. The 'color' of human flesh is created by the many thousands of small arteries and veins carrying blood and oxygen and layer upon layer of tissue and pigment as well. Flesh tone is a translucent 'color' created by these many layers. All of these elements could be thought of as the 'underpainting' of the human figure by which are created what we call the 'flesh tones'.

It is important to bear in mind that the initial washes of color, no matter how often covered over, will influence the final picture. In this case, the artist used a warm, light tone for the underpainting of the figure knowing that this would keep the figure warm in tone, regardless of the colors put down over this initial layer. The white area falling across the figure creates a dramatic contrast to the general dark and sombre tone of the rest of the picture. The square of white in the background is linked with this white area, joining foreground and background and providing unity.

## Materials

Surface
Stretched watercolor paper

Size
21.5in × 14in (53cm × 35cm)

Tools
Nos 4 and 12 sable watercolor brushes
Palette

Colors
| | |
|---|---|
| Alizarin crimson | Indigo |
| Burnt umber | Payne's grey |
| Cadmium lemon | Prussian blue |
| Cadmium scarlet | Rose madder |
| Chrome green | Yellow ochre |

Medium
Water

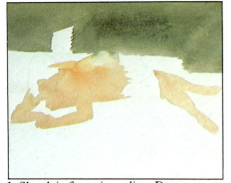

**1.** Sketch in figure in outline. Dampen background area and spread wet mixture of indigo and cadmium yellow. Mix cadmium and yellow and put in figure.

**2.** When dry, mix wash of water and Payne's grey and put in bed. Strengthen tone of paint by adding more grey to create dark shadow areas.

**3.** Mix Payne's grey and cadmium red light in wet wash and put in floor with a No 12 brush, keeping the tone consistent.

**4.** After figure has dried, put in a light wash of rose madder with a No 4 brush letting brush and paint describe the subtler flesh tones.

**5.** Add more red to flesh tone and put in striped shadow area across figure.

**6.** Create darker flesh tone by adding a touch of burnt umber. With Payne's grey, describe shadow area in bed and window. Put wash of yellow over figure.

**7.** Mix a dark shade of chrome green and flood in over the background color with the No 12 brush.

**8.** With a dark mixture of Payne's grey and water, put in deep shadow tones in bed and under figure's feet.

**Using warm wash · wet-in-wet · shadow details**

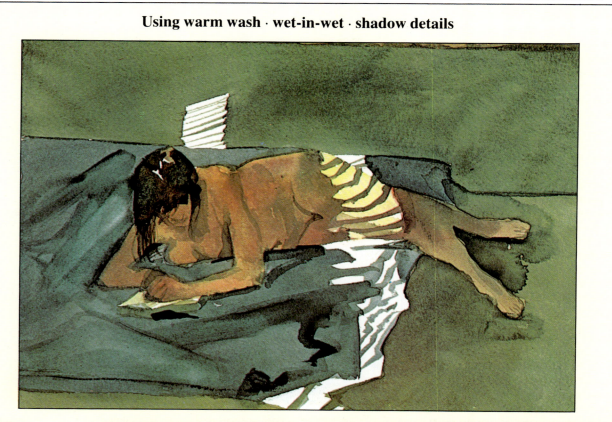

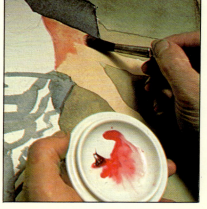

Mixing paint in small dishes which can be held in the hand allows the artist to work quickly. Here the artist is overpainting the initial yellow layer in the figure's legs with a warm red.

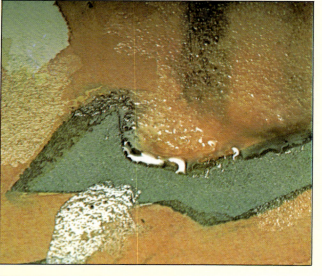

Working over the slightly damp underpainting, the artist lays in thin lines of dark paint to describe the shadow over the figure.

One way of working wet-in-wet is to lay down a small area of color (above) and then immediately flood this with a clean brush and water. If too much water is applied, this is easily lifted with a small piece of tissue or cotton. Remember not to rub into the surface, but simply blot up the excess moisture (left).

# Watercolor

IN THIS PAINTING, thin, transparent layers of watercolor have been laid one on top of another giving the flesh a truly 'flesh-like' feeling and texture. Few other painting media are capable of this effect.

This painting exemplifies many of the more sophisticated ways in which watercolor may be used to create a strong but subtle portrait. The methods used require a steady hand, and familiarity with and confident use of the various watercolor techniques.

The flesh tones of the face, which, from a distance, merge into a continuous area of light and dark, were individually laid down and then blended with a clean, wet brush. Yellow and green were used to render the warm and cool tones of the flesh. The very dark details of the face were described in a strong burnt umber which contrasts with the pale flesh tone and emphasizes their importance.

## Materials

**Surface**
Smooth board

**Size**
16in × 23in (40cm × 57.5cm)

**Tools**
Nos 00, 1 and 2 sable watercolor brushes
2B pencil
Colored pencils

**Colors**
*Watercolor:*

| | |
|---|---|
| Burnt umber | Chrome green |
| Cadmium red | Ultramarine blue |
| Cadmium yellow | Yellow ochre |

*Colored pencils:*
Grey
Red

**Medium**
Water

Watercolor is especially well-suited for portraiture. Because of the inherent transparency of the medium, it is important that the overall image has a strong composition. In this picture, the artist has surrounded the figure with almost empty space to draw the observer's eye into the figure.

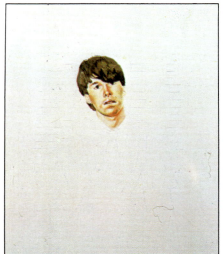

The entire painting progresses from light to dark. Here the artist is putting another wash of color over the hair to create a darker tone.

**1.** Begin by putting in the mid and shadow tones with a thin wash of burnt sienna and green. With a small sable brush and pure umber, add eye details.

**2.** Continue with dark details of the eyes, nose and mouth. If the paint becomes too wet, blot with a tissue and then rework.

Using a strong blue and small sable brush, shadow areas are created in the shirt. Notice how the paint naturally bleeds into the damp surface, creating a gradated tone.

**3.** Apply a thin wash of yellow ochre over the face and work wet-in-wet with a light wash of green in the shadow area.

**4.** Block in the shirt with a thin wash of ultramarine blue. Carry yellow ochre tone into pants leaving white of paper for highlight areas.

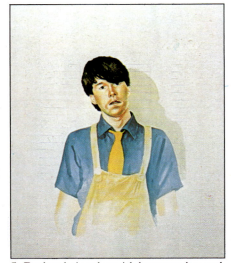

Once the paint surface is thoroughly dry, the artist works back into the face and detail areas with colored pencil, strengthening outlines and shadow areas with light hatching strokes.

**5.** Darken hair color with burnt umber and a fine brush.

**6.** With red pencil, work into the face with very light, diagonal strokes, heightening warm areas. With a grey pencil, strengthen horizontal lines of door.

A QUICK WATERCOLOR portrait may result in an interesting finished picture or may be used as reference for a larger work. This painting shows a lively impression of the overall form of face and figure, lightly modelled with color and tone.

The essence of the technique is to lay the color in watery pools which give the surface a loose, rippling texture. The painting must be allowed to dry frequently to get the full effect of overlaid washes and liquid shapes. It is important to keep the colors bright and true; you need to use plenty of clean water and rinse out the brushes thoroughly after each color application. Start by picking out small shapes of strong tone and color and develop the form in more detail as the painting progresses, drawing separate elements together to construct the entire image.

Since the painting is quite small you need only one brush to lay in the washes, and a finer point to draw up small linear details in the features. Make a brief pencil sketch to establish a guideline at the start but allow the painting to develop freely drawing over the pencil lines with the brush.

## Materials

**Surface**
Stretched cartridge paper

**Size**
12in × 16in (30cm × 40cm)

**Tools**
Nos 3 and 7 sable watercolor brushes
Plate or palette

**Colors**

| | |
|---|---|
| Black | Gamboge yellow |
| Burnt sienna | Scarlet lake |
| Burnt umber | Ultramarine blue |
| Cobalt blue | |

**Medium**
Water

**1.** Work over the hair and face with wet pools of color – scarlet, yellow and burnt sienna – letting the tones blend. Drop light touches of cobalt blue into the shadows.

**2.** Block in thin patches of colour in the background and heavy washes of ultramarine to show the folds in the clothes.

**3.** Strengthen the color over the whole image, developing the structure of the forms. Keep the paint fluid and allow the colors to merge on the surface.

**4.** Model the face with heavy patches of red and brown, drawing in detail around the eyes with the point of a brush. Extend the background color.

**5.** Use mixtures of ultramarine and burnt umber to darken the shadows. Redefine the shapes in eyes and mouth.

**6.** Lay in a black wash across the background to bring the shape of the head forward. Add detail to the forms and strengthen the colors.

## Using paper tone

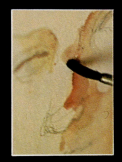

To create face details, the artist runs loose washes of color into one another leaving the paper tone to define highlights.

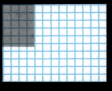

WATERCOLOR IS an excellent medium for painting children. It is delicate and subtle, with light flesh tones and soft shadows evolving gradually through layers of thin, pale washes applied over details.

When painting children, the temptation is often to make them look like small adults. For this reason, details of the pose which are characteristically childlike, such as the roundness of unformed features and smooth skin, must be captured exactly. It is usually easier to work from a photograph as lengthy sittings may be boring for a child. Take several photographs and choose the one which best suits the purpose, or use several in combination as reference.

The range of colors here is limited to shades of red, grey and brown. Blue was added to the browns and greys in the shadow areas to contrast with the overall warm tone of the colors. The image is drawn with the brush over a light pencil outline, first establishing the shapes and tones in the head and moving down to block in the entire body. Details in face and hair are drawn in fine lines with the point of the brush and then overlaid with washes of color. Dry-brush is used to create soft textures by loading a brush with dryish paint and, with the bristles spread between finger and thumb, drawing the brush across the paper to form light, broken strands of color.

## Materials

Surface
Watercolor paper

Size
16in × 22.5in (40cm × 56cm)

Tools
No 3 round sable watercolor brush
Palette or plate

Colors
Black
Burnt sienna          Payne's grey
Burnt umber          Scarlet lake
Cobalt blue           Yellow ochre

Medium
Water

**1.** Work up detail around the eyes with light red, grey and burnt umber using a No 3 brush. Put in strands of hair.

**2.** Show soft shadows under the chin and mouth with light red and Payne's grey. Block in the body with a light wash of grey.

Using the same tone as for the shirt, made lighter by adding water, the artist puts in very pale shadow areas on the face.

To create a dry-brush effect, dip a brush in paint and blot on a towel or rag. Press the brush hairs between thumb and finger to spread the hairs and brush on to the surface with light, feathering strokes using only the tips of the hairs.

**3.** Model the features more clearly with grey and brown washes. Lay in a strong black shadow to one side of the face.

**4.** Draw up the folds and patterning in the blouse with lines and washes of dark grey, drawing with the tip of the No 3 brush.

**5.** Work over the whole painting adding small touches of tone and color, elaborating details with the same brush.

## Finished picture · facial shadows · using dry-brush

The full-faced centred portrait is perhaps the most direct way for the artist to present his subject. If the media and techniques used are handled carefully and thoughtfully, the overall effect can be both strong yet subtle.

THE PAINTING technique used here is loose and fluid and thus suited to the relaxed, informal attitude of the subject. This is basically a simple color study, as the forms are suggested in the brushwork rather than through accurate drawing and meticulous modelling. The figure is emphasized by the strong dark tones of clothes and hair and broad areas of black are enlivened with touches of vivid dark blue, violet and warm browns.

The whole composition is built up by laying in small local shapes and colors, gradually drawing them together into a coherent image. The vitality of this type of study depends upon working quickly, letting the eye travel across the subject to pick out color relationships, and translating them on to the paper with fluid and vigorous brushwork. Keep the brushes well loaded with paint so that each line and shape flows freely on to the paper and the liquid colors merge gently together.

Let the painting dry out completely from time to time so that subsequent color washes are fresh and sharp. If the painting is still wet the fine lines will spread and lose definition.

Small linear details such as the eyes and mouth should be drawn over a dry wash with the tip of a brush.

## Materials

Surface
Stretched cartridge paper

Size
15in × 18in (38cm × 45cm)

Tools
HB pencil
Nos 3 and 7 round sable watercolor brushes
Plate or palette

Colors
| | |
|---|---|
| Black | Scarlet lake |
| Burnt sienna | Ultramarine blue |
| Cadmium yellow | Violet |
| Prussian blue | |

Medium
Water

**1.** Draw the basic shapes in the figure and background with an HB pencil. Wash in patches of strong wet color – black, burnt sienna, violet, Prussian blue and yellow.

**2.** Work into the flesh tones with washes of light red using a No 7 brush. Loosely apply colored shapes over the whole painting to indicate the forms.

**3.** Strengthen the blacks and draw into the pattern of the skirt with a No 3 brush. Bring together the background shapes with blocks of solid color.

**4.** Put in dark shadows on the face and arms with burnt umber and violet. Lay in light washes of blue and green across the background letting the colors run.

**5.** Work on the modelling of the figure with dark tones, defining the details of face and hands. Use muted tones in the background to draw the figure forward.

**6.** Continue to work on the figure gradually developing the tonal contrasts. Draw the features more finely with the point of the brush.

**Finished picture · wet underpainting**

The full length portrait presents the artist with a number of options and challenges and is often more difficult than the head-only variety. Included in the decisions to be made are where and how to place the figure, and how much of the background area to include.

In the initial stages, thin washes of color are laid down to describe shape and form. Note in the figure's hair how the paint has bled outward to create a natural outline.

WHILE THIS painting may prove difficult to think of as a serious watercolor portrait, it expresses some of the most attractive attributes of the medium for the artist.

Despite its humorous aspect, the techniques and composition should not be overlooked. It is largely through the unique placement of the figure and the use of the clean, white space around it which forces the viewer's eye into the face of the subject. The strong darks of the hat and beard contrast boldly with the white of the paper making it impossible for the observer not to look directly into the face. This, coupled with the meticulous control of the medium and light, informal rendering of the shirt, serve to emphasize the focus of the painting.

## Materials

Surface
Watercolor paper

Size
16in × 23in (40cm × 57.5cm)

Tools
2B pencil
No 4 sable watercolor brush
Palette or plate

Colors
Alizarin crimson
Black
Burnt sienna
Payne's grey

Medium
Water

**1.** With a No 4 brush, describe the hat and beard in Payne's grey. Keep the paint very wet and draw in outlines carefully, using only the tip of the brush.

**2.** With same color, define the eyes, nose and mouth. Describe detail of hat in red.

**3.** Work over the face and neck with a darker wash of burnt umber and a touch of red to build up the picture.

**4.** With a thin wash of Payne's grey, lay in shadow area of neck and chest.

**5.** Wet area of shirt with a clean brush and water. Very quickly lay down a wash of light Payne's grey, letting the tones run into the paper and one another.

**6.** While still wet, work back into the shirt with a thin wash of burnt umber, allowing drops to fall from the brush.

**Blocking in color · tones and textures**

Major color areas are blocked in with a thin wash and medium sized brush. Keep the brush moving to avoid building up puddles of color. If too wet, blot with a tissue.

Thin washes of color are laid over one another to build up a surface of varying tones and textures. In the final stages, the artist works with darker tones and smaller brushes to describe face details.

# Gouache

GOUACHE IS a convenient medium for doing quick color studies. It is cleaner to work with than oils and is also more opaque and matt than watercolors or acrylics. The colors are clear and intense. When mixed with white, they form a wide range of bright pastel tints suitable for the skin tones in a portrait. Because the paint is opaque you can work light over dark or vice versa, adjusting the tonal scale of the painting at any stage. The paint is reasonably stable when dry and thin washes of color can be laid over without damaging previous layers.

By studying the head in this painting carefully, the relationships between form and color become apparent. Work in small shapes of color, drawing with the brush to model curves and angles. A loose charcoal drawing is a helpful guideline at the start and can later be used to redefine outlines if the paint is not too thick. Adding black to make shadow areas may dull a color; shadows on the skin usually have a subtle cast of color such as green, blue or purple which can be used instead of black. Contrast these shadows with red and yellow within the lighter tones

## Materials

**Surface**
Stretched cartridge paper

**Size**
16in × 20in (40cm × 50cm)

**Tools**
Medium willow charcoal
Nos 3 and 6 sable round brushes
Plate or palette

**Colors**

| | |
|---|---|
| Alizarin crimson | Cobalt blue |
| Black | Flame red |
| Burnt sienna | Violet |
| Burnt umber | White |
| Cadmium yellow | Yellow ochre |

**Medium**
Water

**1.** Draw the outline of head and shoulders with charcoal, indicating eyes, nose and mouth. Lay thin washes of red and brown to indicate shadows with a No. 6 brush.

**2.** Identify basic colors in the face and neck. Draw out contrasts by exaggerating the tones slightly, overlaying patches of each color to build up the form.

**3.** Draw into face with charcoal and paint in linear details with the point of a No 3 brush in dark brown. Work up the color in and around the features.

**4.** Alter the shape of the head and lay in dark tones of the hair. Paint the stripe pattern on the scarf in cobalt blue and strengthen the red of the jacket.

**5.** Develop the structure and colour of the face, drawing into the features with the No 3 brush and adding thick white and pink highlights with brown shadows in the flesh.

**6.** Block in the hair with a thin wash of yellow ochre and delineate separate strands with burnt umber. Reinforce the shapes of eyes and mouth with small color details.

# Modelling with tone

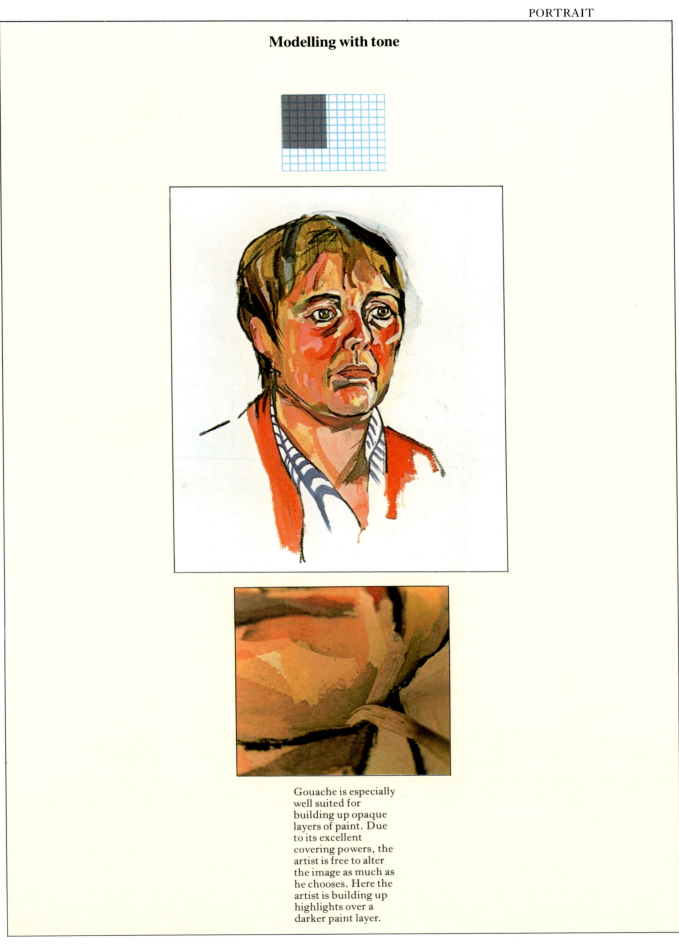

Gouache is especially well suited for building up opaque layers of paint. Due to its excellent covering powers, the artist is free to alter the image as much as he chooses. Here the artist is building up highlights over a darker paint layer.